MY LIFE RECLAIMED

by the Grace of God

Nick Nicholas

Publication information:
My Life Reclaimed: by the Grace of God
ISBN: 978-1-998014-28-6
Copyright © 2024 Nick Nicholas

Print Editing and Layout and e-pub creation:
I. Gaudet, Success Publications

Published by:
Success Publications - division of Creativity
    Corner Inc.
Box 10, Egremont, AB T0A 0Z0
www.SuccessPublications.ca

Photo Credits:
Courtesy of Pdproductions, Paul Dagistano

Chapter One

The Event That Changed My Life

It had been a long day. It was a Saturday and I'd been in a business meeting all day. I got home about four in the afternoon and still needed to spend a couple of hours on a project on which I was working. I sat at my computer working away when suddenly everything started going dark. Not just dimming but encircling me in a dark tunnel. Then I was fully engulfed in the most beautiful light I had ever seen. The feelings of love and peace were overwhelming. I was so at peace I didn't want it to ever end. Then it was gone, and I was once again sitting at my computer feeling full of love and so peaceful.

I continued to work for about an hour and then went into our Arizona room to ask my wife, Darlene, what was for dinner. Off-handedly, I shared with her what happened. There was no more talk about dinner that evening. Within thirty minutes, she had me in the Banner Boswell Hospital emergency room. They poked, prodded, and ran tests but could not find anything wrong with me. Finally, they decided to hold me overnight for observation. Being the weekend, I did not expect much to happen until Monday morning. Boy was I wrong. At six thirty Sunday morning, a technician from Medtronic, the company that supplied my pacemaker, came in to evaluate it. I joked with her asking if I had a heart. She remained stoic and unsmiling. She packed up her gear and left without a word. Immediately, a nurse came in with a bag of ugly yellow medication and hooked it to my IV. She handed me a piece of paper to sign before she could turn it on. The sheet gave all the ways in which this medicine was going to kill me.

I said, "NO, I'm not signing that." Without a word she left the room. Wow, I was doing a wonderful job of winning friends and influencing people.

Not five minutes later, the phone by my bed rang. It was my Cardiologist, and it was not yet seven on a Sunday morning. He said, "Nick, you don't know what happened last night do you?"

I told him, "No I did not."

He then told me that the bottom of my heart seized up and forced all the blood back up through the valves into the upper chamber. He went on to explain that from the second it started, until death, was only thirty-two seconds. My pacemaker pulled me out in twenty seconds. He told me I was only twelve seconds away from death.

I looked at the nurse and said, "Turn that thing on."

As I laid there thinking about what the doctor told me, I realized that he said I was out for twenty seconds, but I knew that I was in that light much longer than that. That is right, time as we understand it does not exist on the other side. Over there it is eternal. The more I contemplated what happened and how I was feeling, the more it became clear to me that my life was now somehow quite different. Other than a deep sense of peace and calm that I'd never experienced before, I wasn't sure what was different.

Little did I realize then just how vastly different my life was to be going forward. Over the next several days, I was fitted with a new pacemaker and defibrillator, and then sent home.

Chapter Two

Who is God?

Thousands of people have experienced a near death experience such as I had. Not all of us experience it in the same way. Some actually die for a brief period, and some even have been blessed to converse with Jesus. There are those who see relatives and friends who have passed away. Then there are many, like me, that are embraced by the Light. Regardless of the kind of experience it was, everyone comes away changed in some way. The one thing we all agree on is the fact that there are no words to describe the peace, the calm, and the love we felt. The result of the experience is different for each of us. For me, the result was that I discovered the mission God had for me. I strongly suspect that is also the case for many of the others that have experienced a Near Death Experience (NDE).

I know some of you will be skeptical of what I share. Some will dismiss it completely, while some will fully embrace it. I totally accept that and am fine with it. You see, God gave us the right of free choice. That means you are free to make your own decision as to what you do and do not believe.

It was about two weeks after I returned home from the hospital that I experienced the first of the many changes and new understandings that I was to encounter going forward. I awoke one morning, and in that twilight zone between fully awake and still asleep, once again I saw the light. No, I wasn't in the Light, I simply saw it. As I gazed at it, I saw a bright strobe come from the light and land directly on my chest. It gave me an overwhelming feeling of love, peace, a deep belief in God, and a strong sense of commitment to a mission that, yet I did not understand. It was a feeling so powerful that I cannot find words to describe it.

All my life, I have heard people ask these questions: Is God a man or a woman? Is He Black, White, or Hispanic? The answer to these questions is a resounding YES! You are all correct. Our carrying cases, our bodies, may look different, but our spirit, which is the real us, is the energy of God's spirit. This is validated by the Bible as it tells us we are all created in His image. We are all His sons and daughters.

At that moment, the answers to many questions came to me. My new-found understanding does not mean that I am better or smarter than everyone else. I am just a regular, average guy. But from that moment on, my belief in God and His love for all of mankind has been deep, unconditional, and unshakable. That day, I also came to understand that God communicates with us through our thoughts and feelings. Since the day I stood in the light, all my understanding about our relationship with God has been given to me through a thought, which generates a feeling of confident belief. Thoughts are a form of energy.

In one of her books, Betty J Eadie explained her second near death experience. In it she recounted communicating with Jesus and that no words were ever spoken. It was all by thought. She would think of a question and the answer came as a thought.

I now understand that God is energy. That is right; He is a superior spiritual energy of pure love. Think about it for a minute; it just makes sense. In the beginning, God created the heavens, the earth, and all living things. Many people prefer to believe in the big bang theory. Both are right. How can that be; it must be one or the other? Nope, not so. God is a superior spiritual energy force. It was His energy that was the big bang. Since He created all things, and He is energy, then all things are energy.

How does this answer the question of how we are all created in His image? It is because His superior spiritual energy of pure love lives within us. That is right, we know it as our emotion of love. In fact, there are only two emotions. They are love and fear (I will talk more about fear later). Our emotions are not really emotions, they are our spirit. They are who we are as a person. Our emotions/spirit motivates our decisions, which in turn directs our actions. Whether our spirit is controlled by love or fear determines how we behave as a person. We have all heard harsh and mean people referred to as mean spirited. We have also heard kind, compassionate, and helpful people referred to as having a loving spirit. The good news is that we can manage our spirit. God gave us that ability. I'll go more in depth on that subject later.

A short two weeks later, I was to experience the next major change in my life.

Chapter Three

My First Encounter,
Becoming My New Normal

It was my first week back at work, and I had several afternoon appointments, but had stopped at a Taco Bell for a quick lunch before my next appointment.

As I sat there eating my tacos and reading my book, I heard someone speak to me. I looked up and this gentleman asked me if I was a priest or a pastor. I told him no.

He then said, "I don't know who you are, but I know I need to talk to you." Then without asking, he sat down at my table.

Later, I realized that as he began to speak, I lost awareness of the noise made by the lunch crowd. My focus was totally on him. Over the next forty-five minutes he shared with me things he had never shared with another person. As he laid out his troubled life, he cried, and he laughed. However, as he spoke, I began to have a full understanding of his problem. No, not how to fix each problem, but rather how he was approaching the decisions he made regarding the challenges he faced. As he finished, he asked the question that moved him to feel the need to talk to me.

He simply said, "How do I fix this so I can live a happy life?" When he finished, I gave him a couple of minutes to collect himself, then I spoke.

This is how I answered his question. I told him that because of all the significant challenges he had faced, he was living in a constant state of fear. I explained that his spirit of fear controlled all his decisions, and that fear blinds us, confuses us, and paralyses us. This makes it nearly impossible to see the full scope of possible solutions. Therefore, it is extremely difficult to make well thought out rational decisions. Because of this, he was unable to see what God was showing him and what to do to achieve the best solution. Because of fear's control of his spirit, he was making decisions without seeing the full range of possibilities. I then shared with him how to change his negative fearful spirit into a God's loving spirit, thus changing how he made his decisions. He got up, shook my hand, thanked me profusely, saying he now knew how to change his life. And with that, he left.

I sat there after he left feeling exhausted. My shirt did not have a dry spot on it, even in this rather cold restaurant. I finally made my way to my car and just sat there. Then it hit me.

Everything that I shared with him was new to me. This left me feeling very concerned. How did I completely understand his situation? How did I know what the solution was? How did I know what information to share? Where did this information come from? I cancelled my afternoon appointments and went home.

When I arrived home, Darlene could tell that something was different and gave me a big hug. We sat at the table, and I told her what happened and that I was concerned about how I knew those things. It was at that point that she told me she thought I should go and share with my priest what had happened over the past several weeks.

Chapter Four

Life Lessons Begin

The following week, I met with the priest and, boy, were my eyes opened. If I thought I was concerned before meeting with the priest, after that meeting, I was really worried.

Father was very understanding as I explained everything that had happened. He asked me to tell him about my life before the incident. This is what I told him.

I explained that I had grown up in a Christian home and was taught the difference between right and wrong, as well as being taught that if you did good things, in God's eyes, you would not experience any negative events in your life. On the other hand, if you did bad things, God would punish you.

For the first fourteen years, that worked well for me, and I had a decent childhood. Then it all changed. In the summer between my junior and senior years of high school, my mom died unexpectedly. She was in the hospital after surgery and was scheduled to come home on Monday. At three o'clock Monday morning the hospital called to tell us to hurry to the hospital as her temperature was extremely high and she had gone into a coma. They did not expect her to live until morning. When we got there, my stepdad went in first, followed by my brother. I was the last to go in. I sat by her bed and held her hand. She had always told me that I would ask her for something while she was on her death bed. She was right, I did. I asked her to get well and come home. I asked God to make her well.

It was then that she squeezed my hand. She turned her head, opened her eyes, looked at me, smiled and took her last breath. I swear I saw movement come from her eyes as she passed away. I later learned that the movement I saw was, in fact, her spirit leaving her body. It has been medically proven that the body losses a quarter of a pound at death.

Of course, I began crying as I was devastated. I asked God what I did wrong that He didn't answer my prayer.

It was many years later that I remembered another situation where God did not answer my prayer. I was about eight years old, and I wanted a BB gun for Christmas. I asked God to let my folks know so I'd get one. Christmas came, and all I got for gifts was clothes. I asked my mom what I'd done wrong; that my prayer was not answered. In her wisdom, she told me my prayer was answered. I was confused as I didn't get the BB gun. She then told me that God answers all prayers. What we don't understand is, that we pray for what we want, and God answers with what we need. As I look back, I wish I'd kept that piece of wisdom in my constant memory.

I told the priest this was not the first time I questioned God. I kept asking what I did wrong that caused Him to punish me by taking my mom from me. If that were not bad enough, five weeks later, I discovered that the girl I thought I'd marry when we graduated from High School was cheating on me with several of my friends. I considered that my second betrayal. At that point I said, "God, that's strike two."

The following September, I went away to college with a new attitude. That attitude was, who cares about being good? God's going to punish me anyway. I went wild. During that year, I met my first wife. Our relationship was off and on during the school year, but in July of 1960, we were married. Over the next eight and a half years we had, what I thought, was a rather good marriage. We had two wonderful children. I had a wonderful job, and all was right with the world. Or so I thought.

Father listened as I continued with my life's story.

Chapter 5

Turning My Back on God

My job required me to travel, and one week I came home two days early, unannounced, and discovered that my wife and a good friend were having an affair. Okay God, that is strike three. I really don't need you in my life anymore. I turned my back on Him and went rogue for the next twelve years and I ran wild. I did what I wanted whether it was right or wrong, and I did not care who I hurt. I considered the ten commandments as merely suggestions. The only one that I did not trample on was, "Thou shall not kill." At one point, my dad told me that I was the best con artist he ever met, and he didn't mean it as a compliment. I'm not proud of the things I did, and I made a lot of bad decisions, but I found a way to justify them. In fact, when I first left my wife, I was homeless for three months. I spent most of that time drunk, chasing women, and just raising hell. If it felt good, then just do it.

At that point, I stopped talking and waited for the priest's response. After a short pause, he said he wanted to hear more about my life up until the time of my being in the light. So, I picked up the story.

Chapter 6

The Beginning of a New Life

It was late November of 1968, when I woke up in an alley in Joplin, Missouri. I was only dressed in summer weight clothes and was freezing. On top of that, I had the mother of all hangovers. I stumbled around the building and went in where it was warm. I followed the smell of fresh coffee and found myself in the U. S. Army recruiting office. Yep, I got warm, got coffee, and got what turned out to be a new life with a great career.

I went into the army with a single purpose, to get trained as an infantryman and get a one-way ticket to Vietnam. Yep, I planned suicide by Viet Cong AK-47. It worked out well. The army sent me to infantry school, and then some special training which taught me to work in a team to gather intelligence on VC movements, as well as any other information we could gather.

During that training, I learned many things, and developed some skills that would become a major part of my later life. One will stay with me for life.

At the end of the special training, there was a field training exercise that required us to use what we'd learned. We were put in teams of three and required to move through ten miles of rough terrain and to collect planted information, as if it were a real operation. Of course, we had an aggressor force. Our aggressor was North Vietnamese soldiers who had been captured and chose to come to our side and train our people.

The first three days of the exercise went very well. As we neared the finish line, we discovered that the last several hundred yards was an open field. We needed to cross that without being discovered. We were nearly halfway across when we were captured. We were then taken to a prison camp.

It was at the POW camp that the "real" learning began. The aggressor's purpose was to torture us to gain information. It was always my belief that torture was to create enough physical pain beyond what you could stand. In fact, this is not entirely true. Yes, it is to create a lot of pain, but the purpose is to bring you to a point where it is bad enough that you become afraid that they will do it again if you don't do what they want. It's a combination of physical and emotional pain. I can truthfully tell you that emotional pain is far worse than physical pain. Their key is to determine what you are already afraid of. So, they do many things to determine which ones really bother you. In my case, at that time, it was claustrophobia and snakes.

Around 0300, or 3 AM, which is our weakest time of the day, they tied my hands and feet and placed me in a wooden box buried in the ground, put the lid on it, and began to cover it with dirt. Within minutes, I felt something crawl across my neck and shoulder. Yes, a snake. I began to panic. They definitely had my number. But this is where I learned a powerful lesson that would play a major role in my life going forward.

Before the exercise, we were given training on ways to avoid reacting to frightening situations. They taught us that we can remove ourselves from situations such as the one I was in now. I couldn't physically remove myself from this situation, but I could remove myself mentally, therefore, changing my emotional reaction to the situation. Changing your thoughts will change your response to the situation.

So, what did I do? I sang the star-spangled banner. Said the Lord's prayer and then thought about the previous weekend in town. I'll not go into detail, but suffice to say, my date and I had a wonderful weekend, and I relived it all in my mind. It was certainly a better place to be than that damn box. When they took me out of the box, I still refused to answer their questions. I later found out that I was buried for nearly an hour. I learned later that changing your thoughts from negative to positive not only changes your response, but it also neutralizes your fear giving you more positive control of your actions.

Chapter 7

God Redirects My Life

Truth be told, a person with a death wish like mine could get a lot of people killed. In its wisdom, the army never allowed me the opportunity to get close to Vietnam.

So, over the first five years of my career, they gave me reasons to re-enlist. At the end of my first two years, I was assigned to the air defense command. I was at Ft. Carson, CO with the 4th Division when I was injured in a field exercise. As a result, I was temporarily assigned to personnel pulling records at the front desk. One day, the Division Command Sergeant Major came in requesting five records. As I turned to get the records, he said to pull mine also. The next day, he came back with three of the records. He told me to put those records back and the other three individuals, me included, were to report to the Brigade headquarters at 1300 hours that afternoon.

Guess what? The army had a brand-new job for me. Yes, I had just been transferred to the U.S. Army Recruiting Command (USAREC). They finally found a job for which I was well suited because of my previous years in sales. The rest of my twenty-year career was spent in the recruiting command. Frankly, I excelled at the job. The first few years, I was a field recruiter. Because of my success, I was assigned to the army recruiting school and spent four and a half years as an instructor. Then I was assigned back to the field to recruit professional nurses. I had only been there a few months when I was sent back to the recruiting school on temporary duty (TDY), to help design and teach a special course for station commanders and captains who were being assigned to command recruiting companies. Little did I realize that with this assignment, my direction in life was going to change in ways that I could never have imagined.

Because of the mass influx of personnel coming to Ft. Benjamin Harrison, we were billeted in the Howard Johnson motel just off post. Several other classes were also billeted at the motel. On Monday morning of my second week there, I was sitting in the restaurant having breakfast with several fellow NCO's. As I looked up, I saw a beautiful strawberry blond, in uniform, walking into the restaurant. I was still in my womanizing days at that time and the instant I saw her I thought, "She's my next conquest."

I was finished eating, so I got up and gave her my chair. This was something I said I would never do for a female soldier. They wanted to be treated like their male counterpart, that's what I'd do. As I was leaving, one of the guys that I knew asked me to get him a carton of cigarettes at the PX.

That evening, I went to his room to give him the cigarettes and guess what? Yes, she was in the room with him. I was devastated, as I thought she had already hooked up with him. The next evening, he invited me to his room to watch the world series game between the KC Royals and the New York Yankees. Again, she was there. However, I learned that they were not together, but were in the same course and he was helping her study for the next day. This was, in my opinion, God putting us together because Darlene was not a recruiter. She requested to attend the Guidance Counselor course to help her with her job of managing the Guidance Counselors in her region. As far as we know, Darlene was the only non-recruiter to attend this course.

The next evening, I had to work late and didn't get back to the motel until after the main restaurant was closed. I decided to go into the lounge and get a hamburger and a beer to take it back to my room. While I was waiting for my order, one of the guys I knew invited me to join him in his booth of four people, two guys and two gals (one who was Darlene, who I had picked to be my next conquest). I sat down next to her, and as I did, we both felt a huge shock; it felt like a

110-volt shock. The guys were staring at us. "What was that?" one of them asked. We saw it all the way over here. When my order came, I invited her back to my room with the full intent of scoring.

I made my best move and got shut down hard. Her answer to my action was a very solid no. I tried again and like the country song said, what part of no don't you understand? After being shut down hard, I did something I had never done before. Instead of throwing her out, we spent the next several hours talking. I shared with her things that I had never told anyone.

Over the next two weeks of her class, we developed a deep and lasting friendship. Yes, we also became lovers. At the end of her TDY we agreed that we would break it off and never talk again, as I was still married at the time. Unfortunately, it was a very troubled marriage. My second wife and I never really developed a good relationship. As I watched Darlene drive away that Saturday morning, my heart broke.

For the next two days I moped around barely doing my job. I could not let her go, so I called her. She told me that she was about ready to call me. From that point on, we talked every day. Then one evening I said, "I love you."

There was a slight pause, and she said, "I love you too."

The rest, as they say, is history. When I arrived home after my TDY, I told my wife I wanted a divorce. All hell broke loose, and for the next three years she fought the divorce.

Chapter 8

Preparation for Life

Of course, nothing in my life has ever been simple. A week later, on Monday morning, I went back to work as a nurse recruiter, I was paged by my battalion commander. He told me that General Connelly was on line one for me. Now at this time, the recruiting command was experiencing a major investigation into recruiter malpractice, headed up by General Connelly. To get a call direct from him was not a good sign. I answered the call with, "Good morning, sir."

His response was, "Good morning, Sergeant, how would you like to be assigned to the Boston recruiting battalion?"

I told him that I'd rather be assigned to the training division at USAREC. Without hesitation he said, "Let me rephrase the question, how soon can you be in Boston?"

Against my wishes, I spent the next fourteen months commanding what was then the second largest recruiting station in the command. The real problem was that my wife insisted on going with me. The divorce started in Boston.

It is important here to take a short time out and explain what I learned because of all that had happened to me from the time I went TDY to Ft. Ben, until I ended up in Lowell, Massachusetts. For many years I had blamed God for all the bad things that happened to me, including the things that I was forced to do that I didn't like. What I learned was that none of this was punishment. It was preparation. That is right, preparation for what I do today.

God has a plan for each of us, but he gave us right of free choice. Unfortunately, we choose to do the things we want, and often those things not only don't match God's plan but end up getting us in deep trouble. Of course, we pray for what we want and when we do not get it, we assume the prayer wasn't answered. Not true, God answered the prayer, but he gave us what we needed, which often is not what we wanted.

Here is what I learned later about my assignment to Boston. Two lieutenant colonels, one who I knew as a major, had been keeping an eye on my career, and they knew that this assignment would enhance my career. They took it upon themselves to tell General Connelly I was perfect for the job in Boston. This, as it turned out, was just the beginning of a string of events that guided my life to where it is today. Yes, God answers your prayers, but with what you need, not necessarily with what you want.

The time in Boston was excruciating for me. I did not want to be there, I did not want to have my soon-to-be ex-wife there, and to top it off, because General Connelly sent me there, nobody trusted me. They thought that I was a spy in the scandal investigation. My drinking became much worse. It was not unusual for me to drink three or four six packs every night. I drank until I passed out.

Monday morning, the sixteenth of March 1981, dawned cold with a miserable freezing drizzle. The trees were bare, and the piles of snow were dirty and ugly. I awoke with my usual hangover and headed off to work. We were living on Ft. Devens and my recruiting station was in Lowell, a thirty-minute drive. I had barely left when it happened. I began to shake. I was sweating profusely, and I had a deep chest pain. I could not get my breath, and I felt like I was going to pass out. I could not drive so I pulled off the road and beat my head on the steering wheel. I was screaming, "I cannot do this anymore!", over and over. With that I fell onto the seat sobbing. I just wanted to die. If I'd had a weapon I wouldn't be here today. Then I heard it. A soft voice saying, "Get help, get help." I sat up, took a deep breath, and like a zombie, I turned around and went back to post. I am Catholic so I went to see the Catholic chaplain.

After I unloaded for an hour, the priest just looked at me and said, "Son your life is really a mess. It is so bad I can't help you. But I know who can," he said as he reached for the phone.

Now, when you are under a lot of stress you have some strange thoughts. I thought, does he have a direct line to God? Crazy, I know, but I was stressed. However, he called the tenth special forces stress center on post. They accepted me. This turned out to be my first giant step to taking back my life and living a life of peace and love.

So, what was it that finally pushed me over the edge? It was not just the crap assignment; it was that my life was making a major change. I was in love with Darlene, but she was stationed at Ft. Gilliam in Atlanta, Georgia, and I was stuck in Massachusetts with a stressful assignment, a wife I fought with every day, and a major drinking problem. It broke me.

I worked with the special force's counselor from March 1981 until April 1982. It helped me a lot. In early April of 1982, the weather had begun to moderate, and the snow was beginning to melt. It made life a little easier. But again, I was about to experience yet another major change in my life.

Chapter 9

A New Challenge Appears

As the commander of a recruiting station, you not only need to work with your recruiters, but the paperwork is staggering. My normal routine was to get to the station at about 0645 and go into my office and do paperwork. One of my recruiters would come in about 0715 and start the coffee.

Again, it was a Monday morning, and I was bent over my desk working when I saw a pair of shiny shoes standing in my doorway. Without looking up I said, "Sarge, don't just stand there, get the coffee started." Then I heard the clearing of a throat, I looked up to see Major General Maxwell Thurman standing there. I jumped to attention knowing that I was in deep dodo.

With a smile on his face he said, "Relax Sarge, just have a seat so we can talk." He then spent the next twenty minutes explaining the reason for his visit. I was to be assigned to the headquarters training division and to a project called JOIN, Joint Optical Information Network. It was a computerized sales system designed to ensure every potential enlistee got the same presentation from their recruiter.

Let me explain what happened. I did not learn about it until after I retired and started my own training and consulting business. I was in the Minneapolis, Minnesota airport heading home after a training program. As I sat there, this gentleman, who looked very familiar, sat down next to me. Turns out it was Caspar Weinberger, the secretary of defense under President Reagan. I asked him where he was headed, and he told me he was on his way to Washington to appear before a senate subcommittee investigating the Iran Contra scandal. He said that then, President Clinton, wanted to put him in prison. But he said the SOB will never succeed. He went on to tell me that it would take at least six months before they could get him to trial. "I'll be gone by then," he said, "I've got terminal cancer and have less than six months to live." We spoke for a while longer, and I discovered why we launched JOIN.

His granddaughter went to see the movie, *Private Benjamin*, starring Goldie Hawn, frankly a very funny movie. She came back and told him he had to see the movie. It was so funny, the recruiter lied to her. She did not get her condominium, she had to march in the rain, and she had a very mean drill sergeant.

The next morning, when he got to the office, he told his aide to get him the trailer to the movie. After watching it, he called the Secretary of the

Army and told him to fix the problem. The Secretary in turn called General Thurman, commander of the recruiting command and said, "Fix it." Thus, the birth of project JOIN.

A few short days after the General's visit, I was at USAREC headquarters. No, my soon to be ex-wife did not go with me. Yes, the Boston recruiting battalion expedited my out processing. They could not wait to get rid of the possible Connelly spy.

The first person I met was Major Bryan. I met him at Ft. Ben when he was a captain and one of the people that I trained to be a recruiting company commander. We had hit it off and are still friends to this day and speak regularly on the phone. He retired as a three-star General.

The two and half years I spent on the project was a whirlwind experience. I was designated as the primary briefing NCO demonstrating the prototype system. I spent more time at the pentagon than I did at Ft. Sheridan.

The year 1983 was very eventful. In May of that year my divorce was finalized. On July 30th, Darlene and I were married at Chapel by the Lake on Great Lakes Naval Training Station. A week before Thanksgiving, JOIN was scheduled to be briefed to the Secretary of the Army and to share all we learned during the beta testing of the system. The briefing was to be conducted by

General Thurman and Colonel Greg. I was there just in case the Secretary wanted to see a demonstration of the system.

Now, the recruiting process is a two-phase process. The recruiting station process and the MEPS, Military Enlistment Processing Station, which is the testing, physical, and the guidance counselor who helps the applicant get their guaranteed job (MOS) and duty assignment. Originally, we had these each on a separate floppy disk but for the Secretary's briefing we had put it all on one.

Early that morning, as we were setting up, the IT guy spilled coffee on the floppy disk. I told him to get me his back up. He said, "I didn't bring one."

So, I told him to give me the latest version of the two floppies.

He said, "I didn't bring them."

We were forty-five minutes from the briefing and there was no software. I dug in my brief case and found a beat up set of floppies. I inserted the first one and it booted up.

As I started to take it out and try the second, the IT guy yelled, "Don't do that. The first one may not reboot again."

"What am I supposed to do if the second does not boot during the briefing?"

His answer floored me, "Wing it, Sarge."

The briefing started and the General and the Colonial shared all the data. When they finished the Secretary looked up and said it looks good, but I will never convince the President to allocate the funds. He said that President Reagan only wanted to spend money on boots and bullets. In fact, he did not even have a computer on his desk.

Now, as I'm in the back of the room praying that I wasn't going to need to do a demonstration. General Thurman says to the Secretary, "Before you go sir, I would like Sergeant Nicholas to demonstrate the system for you." I nearly passed out. As I stepped forward my heart was beating a mile a minute. I knew I was in trouble.

Then I remembered what my wonder wife, Darlene told me before I left for Washington. "Sweetheart," she said, "You are good at what you do; you are going to be great." With that thought, my whole mindset immediately changed. I now knew how the extra point kicker must feel when there are three seconds left on the clock, in the fourth quarter of the super bowl, and a field goal will win the game. Like the kicker, I wanted the ball, I wanted to win. Yes, thoughts are powerful.

I sat down with the Secretary and began the demonstration. After the first half was done, I pulled the floppy out and inserted the second. You could feel the air being sucked out of the room. Everyone there thought the demo was all on one disk. The floppy was taking a long time to boot, and I was getting nervous.

Then I looked at the Secretary and said, "Sir, I have conducted a lot of demonstrations, and I am often asked if recruiters would be afraid of messing up the computer."

Then I said, "You can't hurt it," as I started pounding on the keyboard. It was going beep, beep. Then I said the stupidest thing I could have thought of. "Now, don't pound on it too long, or a long hairy arm will come out of the disk slot and grab you by the throat."

After the words were out of my mouth, I knew I had made a huge blunder. You just do not make smart ass remarks to the Secretary of the Army. The second floppy then booted up and I finished the demonstration.

The secretary slid his chair back looked up at the Colonel and said, "You just bought yourself a system. You will have the funds by the 7th of December." He turned, shook my hand, thanked me for the demonstration and said, "Sergeant, don't let that hairy arm grab your throat." He laughed and left the room.

Before I could fully grasp what had just happened, I was mobbed by everyone in the room. Thousands of dollars had been invested in the development of the system and a lot of careers depended on its approval. After the Secretary left,

Colonel Greg asked me if I was aware of the hand on my shoulder during the demonstration. I told him that I was. He said that it was General Thurman's hand and right after you started the second part of the demonstration, he said to me, "We just got our system you do not need me anymore," and left the room.

Chapter 10

Power Team

In early 1984, Darlene and I were called into the commanding general's office. He told us we were going to Washington to do a demonstration for the Defense Advisory Committee on Women in the Service, (DACOWITS). It was to be a demonstration of how the system made sure all women entering the Army knew exactly what to expect. Darlene was to be an applicant who wanted to jump out of airplanes.

When we were scheduled to start, the chairwoman said we'd be delayed as Nancy Reagan wanted to see the demonstration. No pressure, right? After a very lengthy delay, we were told the First Lady would not be able to join us as she was tied up with Maragret Thatcher, the British Prime Minister. Darlene and I looked at each other and wondered what the hell we had gotten ourselves into.

After we finished the demonstration, Darlene left the room to change back into uniform. I answered questions until she returned. The committee was overwhelmed by the fact that she was already in the Army and that we were married. She then fielded questions and won their hearts. The trip was an enormous success. Not long after that, we were again called into the General's office, and he shared this with us.

It seems that the committee we briefed has a lot of political influence, and they were not going to support President Reagan if he ran for reelection. They did not think he had done enough for women in the military. The General went on to tell us that what he was about to say was classified. (Note: it is no longer classified.)

It seems that morning he had received a call from President Reagan's Chief of Staff with a message to be passed on to Darlene and me. It was a thank you directly from the President saying that because our briefing had been so successful, he was now getting the committees support, and he was going to run for a second term.

Chapter 10

God Works in Mysterious Ways

In December of 1984, Darlene and I were reassigned to the second recruiting brigade on Ft. Gilliam located in Alanta, Georgia. I was still struggling with trust issues and PTSD. One of the NCOs in my section was having some anxiety issues and was sent see a Christian Psychologist. When he came back, he was really pissed off and said he would not go back. I got the name of the doctor and made an appointment for myself. It turned out to be one of my best decisions. I worked with him from March of 1985 until November of 1999.

In January of 1989, I retired as a First Sergeant and started my own training and consulting business. I was also a professional speaker.

Chapter 11

My Mission

When I finished reviewing my life for the priest, I stopped speaking and waited for him to share his thoughts. He paused for a moment, and then responded to all that I had shared.

His first words were, "Your life has certainly been interesting. As I listened to your story, three stories from the Bible came to mind. The first was when Moses asked God, 'Whom should I tell the people that you are?' God replied, 'I am that I am.' That certainly could validate your understanding of Him being energy, as one of the characteristics of energy is that it can neither be created nor destroyed but it can only change form.

"The second is the story about the vine and the branch. The Bible tells us that God is the vine and each of us is a branch. Think about this. After He created the heavens, the earth, and all living things he rested. From that point on, He has accomplished all his work through the branch. There were the prophets, Jesus, the disciples, and now each of us. Unfortunately, our branch is blocked with negative thoughts and feelings such as jealousy, anger, hate, prejudice, and many more. However, in your case what has happened over your life and then being in the Light, your branch has been cleared. Not completely of course, you are still human, and you will still have those at times, but now God can use you to do His work. Which brings me to the final story.

"It is the story of Saul's conversion. Saul was a Roman tax collector and persecutor of Christians. On his way to Damascus to persecute and kill more Christians, he suddenly fell to the ground and was engulfed by a bright light from the heavens. Jesus asked him why he was persecuting His people.

"Saul was blinded by the light and his fellow travelers led him on into Damascus. For the three days, he neither ate nor drank. On the third day, his eyes were opened, and he was a changed man. His name changed to Paul who became an apostle and because of his deep and unshakable belief in Jesus, became very influential in the early history of Christianity. He was best known for his letter writing."

Father paused for a minute before going on. "Now," he said, "Nick, there are some things you need to understand about what is going to happen in your life going forward. First, you must understand your situation is very similar to Paul's, but you are not Paul. Like him, you turned your back on God, and spent years hurting people. Also, you were engulfed by the Light and as a result, your eyes were opened. So, again like Paul, your belief in God and Jesus is deep and unshakable. That is where the similarity ends. Because you were both given a different mission.

"Your mission is what I will call a mission of presence. This means that you must be out around people. Be in their presence. Why, may you ask? Because you are different now and people will know, just like the gentleman in the restaurant. You, of course, don't see the difference, but I do, and others will. You have a look of complete peace in your face, and you project an aura of peace. That is God's peace.

"What you have been given is a truly beautiful and wonderful gift from God. However, there are some rules that you must follow. These are the rules:

1. You are never to approach anyone; they must approach you. This can be hard because you now are very sensitive to people's spiritual energy.

2. People's lives will change because of your interactions with them, and many will thank you for changing their lives. When they do, respectfully tell them thank you, but it was not you that helped them, it was God working through you.

3. Do not try to consciously fix their problem; that is not your job. Just open your mind and

let God share through you what they need to know. Remember, this is about them learning to trust God to guide their lives giving them the strength and guidance to handle life's challenges."

He held my hands and said a prayer of thanks, and our meeting ended.

Chapter 12

Power in our Relationship with God

As I drove home, my mind was running a mile a minute. If I thought I was unsettled before, now I was unsettled on steroids. When I got home, I went into the house and told Darlene about my meeting. I told her I was feeling weak and totally drained. She reached out and gave me a big hug and held me. After a few minutes I felt my strength come back as I began to feel fully restored. We both realized right then that her mission was to restore my energy when I felt fully drained after a coaching session. I'm here to tell you that had she not been there as my rock-solid support, I'd have never made it through the following years.

As of this writing, I've carried out this mission for nine years. I have come to realize so many things that bring into question the validity of what we have been taught over the years and have come to believe. As I said earlier, some will be skeptical, some will dismiss it completely, and some will fully embrace it. Believe me, it will be a challenge to accept some of what I'll share, and that's why Father told me that people must approach me. They must be ready to hear the message. I will tell you again that I am Catholic, but none of what I'm sharing here is trying to sell you on any religion. Today, there are over five hundred different religions. What I'm sharing is to help you better understand your spiritual relationship with God, and how it guides our lives. Don't get me wrong, church and religion are very important because it tells us about our Christian history and outlines God's laws. It tells us what we need to do to be good Christians and live our lives in Christ. It is our spiritual relationship with God that converts that knowledge into the decisions we make and the actions we take in our quest to follow God's plan for us, rather than following the directives of the temporal world in which we live. Let me share a story with you that I believe demonstrates just how powerful our relationship with God really is.

One Sunday morning, in March of 2024, I woke up feeling like I was coming down with a cold. I started treating it as a common cold. However, by Tuesday afternoon I was feeling so bad I went to the little clinic near our home. I was diagnosed with what they called A-flu. It is considered to be one step below full blown Covid-19. By four PM, my temperature was rising, and I was feeling worse. The doctor sent me to the hospital. It was the Tuesday of the State of the Union speech. I remember the first part of the speech but nothing after that until Thursday morning. Somewhere in the night, either Tuesday or Wednesday, I felt myself slipping away. I knew I was dying. As I slipped closer and closer to death, I said, "God, I've been doing Your mission for nearly nine years now and I know I can't come home until it's finished. Does this mean my mission is accomplished and I can come home? I'm ready or are You going to intervene?" That was the last thing I remember until I sat up in bed on Thursday morning feeling like I'd never been sick.

Before my discharge, I had several conversations with the nurses and doctor who treated me. Basically, I was at death's door. The doctor told me she changed her treatment plan to be more aggressive. My doctor also has a strong connection to God and felt strongly that I needed to be saved. Based on what she saw in my X-rays, blood work, etc., she felt that I was not going to survive. But on Thursday morning, I surprised my nurse when I was sitting up and feeling like I was no longer sick.

Here is my conversation with the doctor on that Thursday morning. "You are my miracle." I asked why I was her miracle. "Because the first time I came in to examine you, I looked at your temperature, the x -ray of your lungs, and your age, and I really did not believe that you were going to make it." She said, "I got up to leave and at that moment I looked back at you and said, 'You are different. I don't know how, I don't know why, but you are, and I must treat you differently.' And at that point, I changed the treatment to something I had not done before and instructed the nurses to carry out the orders."

In my conversation with my doctor, she shared that she is a very spiritual person and has a close relationship with God. She strongly believes that God gives each of us certain skills to use to carry out the mission He gives us. She believes that He guides her as a physician. My doctor fully believed that on Wednesday morning, He took control of her and guided her to do what she needed to do to save my life. I shared with her my mission and my relationship with God. There is no doubt that God intervened to save my life. My mission is not yet finished. In fact, that Thursday afternoon I did three coaching sessions. Friday, I did two more and one on Saturday. I went home Sunday morning.

Chapter 13

God's Strength and Guidance

Remember, Father had told me not to approach people, even when I felt their negative spiritual energy. When they were ready, they would approach me. For several months after my visit with him, I was only approached by three or four people every three or four weeks.

In the fall of 2021, we moved from Arizona to the heartland, the state of Missouri. The evening before we were to leave, we went to the Village Inn in Surprise, AZ, one of our favorite places. We wanted to give the young man who always waited a token of our appreciation. I gave him one of my books autographed. Our table was close to a row of booths and next to us sat two ladies. As it turned out, they started a conversation with us. They were a mother and daughter. They asked about the book we gave the waiter, and I explained it to them. The mother revealed that she now beginning to doubt God. It seems that her and her husband had gone to Colorado for a wedding. They got there a day early and stayed in a hotel the night before. When she awoke the next morning, she discovered that her husband had died in the night. Obviously, she was devastated.

She said she missed him so badly that she cried herself to sleep every night. As we spoke, I shared this with her.

God places His spirit in us at our first beat. When we pass away our spirit returns to Him. Since God's spirit lives within you and your husband has once again returned to God that means that your husband also lives within you. When you think of him, you communicate with him through your spirit of love. I suggest that each time you think of him place your hand over your heart, smile, and sense his physical presence.

As we finished her daughter left to pay the bill and Darlene went to the lady's room. The woman stood and hugged me tightly. She whispered, "Thank you so much. You have shown me how to connect with my husband and have restored my faith in God."

I told her, "Thank you, but please understand that it was God working through me that healed you." She had a huge smile on her face as she left.

Today, nine years later, I'm approached at least once or twice every time I go out. I've been approached in the supermarket, the pharmacy, on the street, the doctor's office and even in the operating room while being prepped for surgery. Over those years, I've been hospitalized a total of six times, and every time I am approached at least once a day. In the beginning, it was by people like the gentleman in the restaurant who had a specific problem. Today, it's people who claim to have been lifelong Christians, and because of the situation our county is in, are starting to doubt God and want reassurance that He is real and that He will take care of them.

Let me share what I believe is probably the strangest time I was approached. Several years ago, I was in the operating room being prepared for a three-hour surgery. I was sitting up on the operating table with the head nurse holding my shoulders so I wouldn't fall from the table. She looked in my face and asked me if I was anxious or frightened about the surgery. She said, "I see a peace and calm in your face which is something we seldom see in the OR."

I told her, "No, I wasn't at all anxious or frightened."

"Why?" she wanted to know.

I said, "Well, fear is the only thing that can destroy peace. Once we learn to manage fear, we live in peace."

"How do you manage fear?" she wanted to know.

"Please understand that the emotion of fear is, in fact, your negative spirit. Frankly, it is Satan's weapon that he uses to cloud our minds and turn us against God. However, to learn to manage fear, we need to put it into terms which we can use. So, look at it like this; fear is a question. That question is, am I going to be all right, will I survive? We usually answer it with either a 'no' or 'I don't know.' Both are negative thoughts. The true answer is, yes, you are going to be okay, and you will survive. You will find a way to handle it, just like every other time in your life. It may not be the way you like, but you will survive."

She asked me how I could be so sure of that. There are two reasons, one is we will always find a way to survive: it's our human nature. The second, and most important, is that God's spirit is living within you and is constantly, minute by minute, hour by hour, preparing you by giving you what you need to handle the next minute, hour, day, or year. Once we say to ourselves, bring it on, I'm going to find a way to handle it, fear is neutralized. Then you will be able to see God's solution to your situation.

"Before I was brought back, I simply had a conversation with God and told Him I was putting myself in His hands, and the hands of the medical team working on me. That changed my spirit from negative to positive. So no, I'm not anxious or frightened."

With a tear in the corner of her eye she whispered, "I needed to hear that today."

Chapter 14

Projecting God's Peace

It was about two months after my meeting with Father, that a work colleague asked if we could meet for coffee. I arrived at the coffee shop early and when she walked in, I knew she was very troubled. We started our conversation with small talk. Then I asked her if she wanted to share what was bothering her.

She took a deep breath and began her story. It seems that her husband of many years, had cheated on her with her best friend. If that wasn't bad enough, they both basically rubbed it in her face. She was devastated and had completely lost all confidence in herself and her ability to trust anyone. She felt that she had failed as a wife and that as bad as it made her feel, she was taking all the blame for the breakdown of her marriage. To sum it up, she felt helpless, useless, and scared of what her life would be like going forward. She had no family close by, and her friends had backed away, not wanting to get involved.

As she sat there quietly crying, I reached out and took her hand and said, ''You are a very special person. Understand, you are not responsible for the actions of others. You see, we can't control what other people do. They are responsible for their own decisions and the consequences they cause. I understand exactly how you are feeling because my first wife and best friend did the same to me. I learned that as one door closes another door opens to something much better. This is God's way of helping us grow stronger spiritually and directing our lives in accordance with His plan for us.

"All the feelings you are having now, rightly so, are very negative, and they are generating the emotion of fear. Fear is certainly to be expected when it seems your survival is being threatened. Fear is the natural reaction when any area of our survival is threatened. The key, however, is not to let that first reaction continue to control your life. As time passes you will decide to either let this incident control your life or you will decide to refuse to allow that to happen, learn from it, and move on. Of course, the big question is, how to do that when you are in a state of confusion and hurt.

"What I'm about to share with you is a technique I learned from my Christian coach, and then came to understand the spirit of it after being in the Light. The emotion of fear is our negative spirit. God's love, of course, is our positive spirit. Our thoughts direct our spirit, and our spirit controls our decisions, which determine our actions. Therefore, to ensure that our positive spirit, God's love, controls our spirit and our lives we must learn to control our thoughts. Let me give you an example.

"In August of 2010, my dad passed away and we no longer had the financial responsibility of his care, as we had for the past eight years. Frankly, I was burned out from constant travel, so I decided to leave my speaking, training, and consulting business and find something local. To accomplish this, we needed to take a second mortgage on our house. Since we had over two hundred thousand in equity, the bank was excited to make us the loan until the house, which had been appraised a year previously at over four hundred and thirty-five thousand dollars, was now appraised at one hundred and forty-eight thousand dollars. So instead of the two hundred thousand in equity we thought we had, we were upside down by forty thousand dollars. By a week before Christmas, we were desperate as everything we'd tried to do to fix the situation, failed. We were thinking very negatively playing the '*what if, I shoulda, I coulda*' game.

"Since we had no idea what to do next, we sat at our kitchen table and said a prayer asking for strength and guidance. The prayer changed our thinking from negative to positive. After a few minutes, Darlene said, 'I think we should step back from this and go to Phoenix next week and see my folks for the holiday.' The minute our thinking went from negative to positive, our positive spirit, (God's love) took over and the fear was neutralized. Darlene was given God's answer as to what we should do. Before that, there was no thought of going anywhere.

"On our third day at her folks, Darlene came to me and said she thought we had a problem, and I agreed. Her folks were aging and needed help. We decided to leave Florida, and in the first week of February, we relocated to Sun City, Arizona.

"In the end, we may have lost everything... what was left of our savings, the house and the car. The fact is, we were among the thousands that were wiped out by the financial crash of 2008-2010. But we gained a lot too.

"The point of this story is that as we prayed that evening, we turned it all over to God. He then threw a thought and told Darlene what we needed to do. As it turned out, this event changed the direction of our life for the better. We began a new chapter in our lives. A new beginning that led us to a wonderful understanding of our spiritual journey.

"Always remember, you are one of God's special people, and He only wants the best for you even though we must sometimes face very difficult challenges to achieve His reward. What

I'm recommending is that you simply sit down and have a conversation with God. Be honest, just tell him you don't know what to do, don't ask for specific things that you think will help you, instead just ask Him to give you guidance and strength. It will change your thinking to positive and the answers will come. These conversations that Darlene and I have with God around our kitchen table have for our nearly forty-five years together given us the strength and guidance to handle the many hard times, strengthened our marriage and deepened our love for each other."

The next time my friend and I got together was when she walked into our next meeting. She was smiling and was like a different person. Again, after some small talk, and getting our coffee, she said, "I want to tell you a couple of things. The first is that I did as you suggested and sure enough my thinking changed. I began to see other ways to handle this problem. I felt like a huge load had been lifted from my shoulders. The second thing is, do you remember I told you I no longer trusted anyone, especially men?" I nodded and she continued, "Well, we had talked for about five minutes, and I trusted you so much, I'd have done anything you told me to do."

"Whoa," I responded, "that's quite a change. Can you share with me why you felt that way?"

She said, "When I sat down, I was immediately overcome with a deep feeling of calm and peace. I saw peace in your face and heard it in your voice. Whenever I'm in your presence, I feel so calm and peaceful."

I was truly moved by her statement. Then I remembered what father had told me. I smiled at her and said, "What you are seeing, feeling, and hearing is God's peace coming through me. All the changes you have made and will make as we go forward with our coaching, is God working through me to give you His healing power."

We continued to meet for several months, and she continued to build her confidence. She became calmer and more peaceful. She began attending church again. She met and married a wonderful man, and they are still happily married after several years. It is so wonderful what happens in our lives when we put our lives in God's hands.

Chapter 15

When we were born, God gave each of us two missions. The first one is the same for all of us, grow spiritually while you're here in this life. The second one is specifically just for us, and everyone is different. He also gave each of us a special skill or ability, and then, over the years, He prepares us to use that skill or ability to achieve the mission He gave to us. Before I go into detail to explain what this really means to us, there are some things I need to explain so you can better understand why life works the way it does.

As I've shared earlier, our spirit is who we are as a person. To the best of my knowledge, at least for me, no one has ever taught us what this really means. One of the first things I came to fully understand, after that morning the strobe of light came into my chest, is this. Our first heartbeat is God's spirit entering our physical body and we become a living person. It's important to recognize that our spirit is real and guides our life. Our body is basically a carrying case, a physical being that allows us to perform the actions directed by our spirit. Our mind is designed to gather information and learn, then direct the body to act on that knowledge as directed by our spirit. It is very important that we accept that our spirit resides in our heart. Here is a rather simple example of how the body, mind, and spirit work together. We each have five senses. They are touch, taste, sight, smell, and hearing.

As we go through our daily routine, we are in constant contact with our surroundings through those senses. What we perceive through the senses instantly becomes a thought, either positive or negative. Those thoughts instantly generate a feeling, either positive or negative. Those feelings are connected to our positive or negative emotions. Those emotions are, in fact, our spirit which directs our actions. Our spirit is who we are. We've all heard people being referred to as being mean spirited or kind spirited. We are our spirit.

Here is a personal example. I'm a huge Kansas City Chiefs fan. Unfortunately, for many years they had a way of losing critical games. Several seasons ago, they were locked in a tough struggle with a fantastic Buffalo Bills team, in a very important game. Kansas City was down by three points and deep in their own territory with only thirteen seconds left in the game. Realistically, any chance of them winning was slim to none. With their past track record, they were going to lose the game. I was angry and wanted to throw something. My thoughts and feelings were very negative as was shown by my actions. No, I didn't throw anything; instead, I yelled, cursed, and snapped at my wonderful wife. Not a good way to maintain harmony in the home.

As I watched, along with thousands of other people, I was astounded at how Patrick Mahomes drove the team into field goal range with only a few seconds left on the clock. As the field goal kicker walked onto the field, my thoughts took me back to the day I briefed the Secretary of the Army. Like that kicker, I wanted the ball. Those positive thoughts changed my spirit from negative to positive. The field goal was successful and tied the game. Everyone watching, including the announcers, was absolutely stunned. The Chiefs went on to win the game in overtime. I apologized to my wonderful wife for my outburst and celebrated the victory.

Thoughts control our feelings. Those feelings determine if our spirit will be positive or negative. In turn, our spirit determines what decisions we make. Since we think of our spirit as emotions -- love or fear, and since all decisions are made emotionally first, our lives are directed by either love or fear.

Obviously, decisions made from love, our positive spirit, normally have a better outcome than those made of fear. I'll talk more about fear in a later chapter.

In 2012, a year after I closed my training and consulting business, I began doing coaching for small business and entrepreneurs. Prior to December of 2015, I helped many of my clients make minor changes to how they approached business and made suggestions on ways to expand their market. When I started one of our sessions with a client in 2016, it was obvious that the client was extremely stressed and very upset. After a few minutes it became obvious to me that we were not going to accomplish anything until he could calm down.

I said, "Andrew, I can see that you are very stressed and upset. Please share with me what is bothering you." He then went into detail about how bad things were going with his work. He told me he didn't see any way to make it better. He was frustrated and angry.

I told him to close his eyes and take several deep breaths. He began to relax physically. When he opened his eyes, I could tell he was still upset and thinking negatively. I said to him, "Think back over your life and tell me if there is an event that was so wonderful that you wished every day of your life could be like that?"

"Oh yes", he responded. I asked him to share it with me. Here is what he told me. He said, "I'm French Canadian and speak fluent French. A while back I took my wife on vacation to France.

We didn't go as tourists; we spent our time in the economy. We involved ourselves in the everyday life of the French. We ended our trip with several days in Paris. It was a fabulous vacation." As he was talking, I could see the stress and worry leave his face, being replaced by a big smile, "What happened?" he asked.

I told him, "You left our meeting and went on vacation in France with your wife".

He said, "I feel light as a feather and totally relaxed, what did you do?"

Let me explain. Remember my story about being buried alive in a box with snakes, and how I mentally removed myself from the situation? That is what Andrew did. Here is why it works and is so powerful. Every event in our life is stored in our memory in a living color video. Attached to each video is an emotional/spiritual soundtrack. In this situation, it was a positive emotion/spiritual soundtrack. This meant that his thinking went from negative to positive, those positive thoughts changed his physical and emotional/spiritual state to positive.

Here is what I told him. "Reduce that event to one or two words which will always trigger your positive being".

Immediately, he smiled and said "Paris." He was so serious about making the change, he went out and bought a small replica of the Eiffel Tower and put it on his desk. He moves it regularly, so it does not become just part of the furniture. That meeting was eight or nine years ago. We still work together, and that one event has changed his life significantly, including his business. Why? Because he now makes his decisions from the positive spirit instead of the negative spirit. Over the years I've shared this information with hundreds of people, and everyone has experienced some positive change in their life. In all cases, it changed the preponderance of their decisions to be made from their positive, God's love, spirit rather than from their negative spirit of fear. I'll talk more about the spirit of fear in a later chapter.

Chapter 16

So far, I've talked a lot about our spirit and how it directs our lives. Let me explain it in a way that you can make it more visual.

Imagine the heart as it is in pictures or those nice red emoji's ♥. Now, imagine a line drawn vertically from the top to the bottom, dividing it exactly in half. The left side of the picture is rather shadowed while the right side is very bright. The shadowed side is your spirit of fear while the right side is the spirit of God's love. Realize that it is true, that God is alive within you and is constantly attempting to guide you to act in ways that demonstrate love, compassion, and caring. Following His guidance takes you on a path that provides a life of positive thinking and peace, even in a world of total chaos such as we live in today.

Remember the bible story where the disciples were at sea with Jesus asleep in the bow of the boat. A storm came up, but they were unafraid because they trusted Jesus to keep them safe. However, as the storm grew worse, they became very concerned because Jesus had not stirred. As the storm reached the apex of its intensity, Jesus still did not arise and calm the storm. They were now frightened to the point of panic. It was then that Jesus stood and calmed the sea. Often, we fail to grasp the spiritual meaning of these stories. The intellectual learning is that Jesus is very powerful. The true meaning, however, is that no matter how catastrophic the storm in our life is, when we keep our trust in Jesus, he will calm our spirit, negate our fear, and give us internal peace. We may remember this intellectually but why is it so hard to do when we feel like our existence is being threatened? The answer is simple. Satan's fear spirit spurs us to believe that we are going to perish. How then do we combat this and maintain out unshakable trust and faith in God? We can only accomplish this by neutralizing our spirit of fear. I'll go into detail in a later chapter about fear, how it controls us and how to neutralize it, and find the courage to break away from its hold on your life.

Remember, I said earlier that each thought changes your spirit. What this means is that when your thought is positive, the spiritual energy of love moves that line to the left, meaning that your positive thought converted negative fear energy to positive, God's love energy. Here is an example of what I mean. You wake up one morning and think thank goodness it's Friday and it is a beautiful spring day. You are smiling and happy with very positive thoughts which are converting your spiritual energy, thus giving God's love greater control of your spirit. That dividing line moves to the left. Your day starts with a positive attitude and directing your actions from a positive spirit/emotion. It's going to be a great day and a great weekend. You go into work smiling and greeting everyone joyfully.

Then, someone says, "The boss wants to see you." When you walk into their office you are told that because of a deadline you will be working over the weekend. Immediately your thoughts turn negative, and your spiritual energy goes negative moving that line back to the right as your spirit is now negative. This means your decisions and actions are being directed by negativity. Therefore, your life is now being directed from a negative perspective.

Think about it, how many thoughts do we have in a day? Obviously more than we can count, however, every one of them changes our spiritual energy. We've all heard the saying, good days and bad days. Now we know why. One negative event will usually ruin our day. Why? Because we tend to dwell on what happened and our spirit stays negative. That is unless you use the technique I shared with Andrew. I suggest you do as Andrew did and find that one wonderful event in your life and put it into one or two words. Every time you feel upset in any way, say those words and your entire attitude will change and you feel much better. You can turn a bad day into a good day with just one or two words. You may be saying to yourself, well you understand all this, so you never have a problem. Oh no, I'm just like you. I have my share of negative thoughts and bad times. So, let me tell you my spirit changing story.

As you read earlier, I've had some negative years in my life, and negative thinking consumed me. Frankly, thinking negative is very natural for us. When I catch myself feeling frustrated and upset, I just say to myself, "My wedding." I immediately see my beautiful wife walking down the aisle, on her father's arm, coming to me for our vows. Oh, sorry I guess I just left you for a few minutes.

This short reprieve is critically important because it neutralizes fear for a time and allows us to make positive decisions.

It would be wonderful if we had all our spirit to work with every day. Unfortunately, that is not the case. Some of the events we experience early in our life are so traumatic they become permanent. These events impact how we develop our self-image.

Let me share another personal story that created my self-image. As I said earlier, I grew up on a farm in Kansas in the 1940's and 1950's. We never had much money, and when I changed to the city school, I was immediately identified as a poor hick farmer. I was laughed at and was never really accepted as part of the A-list crowd.

That situation, when added to my three betrayals in my early years, gave me this self-image. *You are unworthy, unlovable, and you will never measure up.* Fortunately, over the years, I have been able to change that image because of the work I did with my Christian coach and my new understanding of my relationship with God. I now see myself worthy, loveable, and successful about ninety five percent of the time. However, some of my old self-image remains. Of course, how we see ourselves impacts our thoughts, which in turn direct our spirit. Negative spirit results in negative actions which reinforce our negative image.

Self-image is important because it is who we perceive ourselves to be. If we see ourselves in a negative way, our actions must support that image, otherwise, we become uncomfortable, distrustful, unsure of ourselves, and sometimes, even fearful.

Here is my personal example. Because of those early events in my life, I never developed an understanding about finances and was constantly in financial trouble. If that wasn't bad enough, my lack of trust in anyone or anything, I rejected a lot of good advice. I'd love to tell you that I'm completely over all that, but I can't. Don't misunderstand me, it only has control of me about five percent of the time. Occasionally, it rears its ugly head, and I must use all of what I've learned to get past it. Sadly, when it strikes, I am prone to negative behavior. The good news is that it no longer controls my life. When I met Darlene in 1980, fear controlled over eighty five percent of my life.

Chapter 17

Remember, when we were born, God gave each of us two missions. The first one is the same for everyone. Grow spiritually while here on earth. The second mission was just for us, and He gave us a special skill, talent, or knowledge to accomplish that mission.

What does it mean to grow spiritually, and what role do our challenges play in our preparation and our growth? Let me explain. Everything the Bible tells us is important but, there are two things that are critically important in our spiritual growth and our achieving God's mission for us.

First, God gave us right of free choice. Now He doesn't care what kind of car you drive or job you have. This is what the right of free choice really means. As I said earlier, all decisions are made emotionally/spiritually first; our two emotions, love and fear, are our spirit; and they define who we are as a human being. So, the right of free choice means this, every decision we make is a choice, and that choice is between a decision made from Satan's fear or out of God's love.

Let me give you another example. At work, you must make an important decision. Since there are consequences to all decisions, you look at all aspects of the situation. As you look at it, you know that if you decide not to comply, it could affect your job and might even get you fired. In other words, not complying presents a perceived threat to your professional survival. You also know that in not complying, it is the right thing to do. It's one God would condone. Complying is wrong, but you have a family, and you need your job, so you decide to go along with the situation even though you know it's not the right thing to do. The storm of your professional life, like the storm experienced by the disciples, has reached its apex and you lose your faith that Jesus will save you. However, like the bible story, Jesus will not let you down. Maintain your faith, do the right thing, and it will work out for good just the way God intends for it to.

The Bible tells us is that our battle here on earth is not of the flesh but, rather of the spirit. This is the battle the bible is referring to. The struggle we face is in making those tough decisions. The example I just gave is what the Bible is telling us. The decisions we make, and the actions we take, should be because we believe it is the right thing to do, not because we are afraid of consequences.

The second is to realize that the challenges we face are not punishment, but rather God preparing us for our mission. Let me give you an example.

When I became homeless, I said to myself, "Well, it can't get any worse." I suggest you never say that, because as soon as I said it, guess what? Things got worse and continued to get worse for many years. It got so bad that on many occasions I would look to the heavens and say, "God, what did I do to piss you off? I know You said You'd never give us a load to carry greater than we had the strength to carry, but this is getting ridiculous. Could you just lighten up a little?"

Only later did I come to understand that by dealing with each of those nasty challenges my spirit quietly grew stronger, and what I learned from each one helped prepare me to do what I do today. I've found that people I work with feel much more comfortable with me when they know I've experienced the same or similar situations and found a way to handle it. When I work with someone that has an addiction or has been badly betrayed, they connect with me because I've been an alcoholic, and I've experienced betrayal. Let me share another story with you. I don't know if it happened, but it clearly makes my point.

A young soldier fell into a deep hole and was struggling to get out. Finally, he started yelling for help. A senior NCO came by and told him to keep digging, he'd find a way out. Later an officer came by and told the soldier to just do what his senior NCO told him to do. At this point, the poor guy was exhausted and felt nearly hopeless. Later still, an old soldier came by and seeing the situation jumped into the hole, The young soldier yelled, "Why did you jump in here with me, now we're both trapped."

"Relax," said the old soldier with a smile on his face. "I've been in this hole before and I know the way out, follow me."

What was the lesson that the young soldier should learn from this very difficult challenge? What is the lesson we should also learn from each of the difficulties we face in life? Well, the lesson is simple, however, its execution requires trust and faith. You will learn the answer in a later chapter. I know, I don't play fair sometimes. LOL.

Chapter 18

The first thing I learned after standing in the Light was, that God is a superior spiritual energy of pure love. Of course, we all know that all energy has specific characteristics. It can neither be created nor destroyed. It can only change form. In physical energy, it can change from potential to kinetic. Oversimplified, that means energy at rest has potential for action and energy in action is kinetic.

Spiritual energy, on the other hand, can only change between being positive or being negative. What I've come to understand, and deeply believe, is that the positive spiritual energy is God alive within us constantly giving us strength and guidance. Negative spiritual energy, however, is fear which is Satan's weapon which he uses to seed our minds with doubt and destroy our faith in God. It's important to understand that God's spirit is pure love and is incapable of fear, deceit, or subterfuge. Satan's spirit, however, is governed by no rules and will be cunning, untruthful, deceitful, and present itself as the good guy. We've all heard of a wolf in sheep's clothing and experienced a person who pretends to be a friend while stabbing us in the back. The fact is fear will blind you from seeing God's love, direction, and guidance. It will confuse you with misleading information which clouds your decisions, and finally it will paralyze you and prevent you from acting.

As I said earlier, negative thoughts generate some level of fear. Why? Because our basic instinct is survival. In fact, a man named Maslow listed a basic hierarchy of five needs: physiological (survival), safety, love and belongingness, esteem, and finally self-actualization.

It is our instinct of survival that I want to address. First, the instinct of survival goes beyond life or death which is how most of us view it. The truth is that we have an instinct for survival in every area of our lives: relationships, occupation, finances, overall wellbeing, etc. Anytime there is a real or perceived threat to any one of those, fear is the automatic reaction. For example, there is a rumor around the office that there are going to be layoffs. Immediately, everyone's instinct of job survival is potentially threatened. In fact, several areas of survival are threatened. If you've ever been in this situation, you know that people's demeanor changes, trust begins to wane, and the work environment becomes difficult, if not hostile, until the threat is resolved.

Remember that the fear generated by negative thinking drives negative decisions. However, the deeper your faith and belief in the fact that God will not let you down, the lower your level of fear.

Let me give you a personal example. It's rather simple, and no doubt you will see it as foolish. In 1983, while Darlene and I were stationed at Ft. Sheridan, IL we went to an amusement park. She wanted to ride the roller coaster, but I refused. Here I was, a forty-one-year older soldier, afraid to ride a roller coaster. Finally, she convinced me to try it, I think she shamed me into it. The line was long, and the wait was nearly thirty minutes. Those thirty minutes seemed like hours to me. My hands were sweaty, my mouth was dry, and my blood pressure was probably off the chart. Then we were in the car and moving towards what I saw as the fatal drop off. As we went over the edge, I lost my breath and screamed along with everyone else but held on for dear life. The first thing I said to Darlene after the ride was let's go again. And we did, three times, I think.

Yes, fear causes us to interpret our physical reaction in a negative way which only increases our level of fear, negatively impacting our ability to act. However, I've learned that the physical reaction to fear is the same physical reaction we have to excitement. Excitement generates positive energy causing us to interpret the physical reaction as positive spurring us to action. A lot of failures are caused by fear. Some even say that the greatest reason for failing is fear of the change that success will bring. I'm inclined to agree. I've had several clients who have sabotaged their chance to reach a particular success goal.

Chapter 19

Forgiveness

As Jesus hung on the cross after being scourged, whipped, tortured, and crowned with a crown of thorns you would think He would hate his tormentors and wish them harm. But no, He called out to God, "Father, forgive them for they know not what they do."

How many of us would be able to follow Jesus' example?

My guess is either none or very, very few. In fact, it seems we find it difficult to forgive those who slight us in any way. You know my story and I can tell you that forgiveness was not on my agenda. Revenge, oh yes, that's the ticket. Sadly, in today's world the latter is the norm.

I must admit that at that time I was totally estranged from my biological father and honestly, I'm not sure what I needed to forgive him for as he had never treated me badly. It must have been spurred by the bad relationship between my mom and my stepdad after the divorce. By the time I had my crash in 1981, I felt like I wanted revenge on everyone who had slighted me in any way, including my dad, and especially my ex.

I'm certain that it would be safe to say that all of us have someone in our lives that causes us a lot of anger, distrust, and keeps us pissed off. We know Jesus told us we need to forgive them, but how many of us can truly feel they can do that. Here is something I learned from my Christian coach, and it was later reenforced after standing in the Light.

There are two levels of forgiveness. The first is temporal which is intellectual. This means that if you slight me, I say to you, "Oh, it's okay I forgive you." This gives me the opportunity to say to myself I just did the Christian thing, the right thing. Unfortunately, the next time someone mentions your name I remember the slight I relive the event in real time and get angry all over again.

The second level of forgiveness is spiritual. This means that I forgive you from my spirit. I let go of the negative emotional/spiritual feelings toward you, which were generated by the slight and convert that spiritual energy to the spirit of love. The Bible tells to love our enemies and to turn the other cheek. Wow, can you imagine a world where we are all able to live in complete peace and harmony? We pretty much believe this is a Pollyanna pipe dream and impossible. In my opinion it is only impossible if we never learn to forgive spiritually. I'm not sure we even know what it means to forgive spiritually. To the best of my knowledge, we've always been told we need to do it but have never been shown how, at least in a way that we can understand and practice. Let me share with you what I've learned both from my work with my coach and had validated by my new relationship with God.

As I mentioned earlier, every event in our lives is stored in our mind in living color video. Also, each event generated an emotional/spiritual response which remains attached to the video of that event. As we move through life our five senses are constantly feeding our thoughts and those thoughts trigger past events in our life. For example, when I hear the song, *On the Road Again* by Willie Nelson I immediately remember my first date with my wonderful wife Darlene. We went to a movie starring Willy Nelson, and that was the opening song. It went on to become one of our favorite songs. I still get goosebumps and my heart sings when it plays. Of course, the spiritual connection to that event is very positive. The good news is I get to live it again in real time because my mind doesn't distinguish between past and present. Okay, I relived it as I wrote it, so sue me. LOL.

Unfortunately, the same is true of negative events. Here is one of my examples. When I hear the song, *A Summer Place* by Percy Faith, I immediately remember my first wife and how that relationship ended, a very negative event. I used to relive the terrible event in real time every time I heard the song. Now, I only see the video. The negative emotional/spiritual energy connected to it is gone. This is why we say I'll forgive you, but I'll never forget. This is because the video is a permanent part of our memory.

Okay, how do we achieve spiritual forgiveness and why do bad events connected to my mother's death, my high school sweetheart's betrayal, my first wife's cheating, and all the other slights I've experienced over the many years no longer upset me?

The answer is that I've learned a process to eliminate the emotional/spiritual energy connected to each one of them. I use this process to this day, as the threats and slights keep coming. In fact, in today's world, 2024, I am using it much more often. Let me share an example. I think we can all agree that right now our world is in a state of complete chaos. Everything that we've counted on for our safety and the safety of our families has been turned upside down. Some even refer to it as being weaponized.

It doesn't take a rocket scientist to realize that these changes are the result of decisions and actions of our leaders from the local level all the way to Washington D.C. It would be easy for us to have feelings of anger, frustration, and hate for these people. Yes, I feel angry and frustrated, but I can't hate someone that I've never met and don't know. What I do hate is the actions they take that seem to deliberately make my life more difficult and less safe.

However, I realize that I have neither control nor influence over their actions. Therefore, I can either run around upset all the time or I can control my response, which is the only control any of has. I use the process I'll share to make it possible for me to accomplish this. The bottom line is that we must disconnect the negative emotional/spiritual energy from the event. There are several ways to accomplish this. Most, however, require the assistance of a professional psychologist or psychiatrist. There is one that you can do yourself at home. My coach taught me this one so I could continue to forgive going forward in my life. I'll share it with you as I experienced it with my coach.

At the end of one of our sessions, he asked how I felt about my mother. I told him that her death was so many years ago I don't even remember. Then he gave me this homework assignment. He told me to sit quietly and think about her and then using a pen and paper, no computer, write her a letter telling her how her death made you feel. Only write about feelings, not thoughts or actions.

The next day I sat down to do my homework. As I started writing I was amazed at the awful feelings I was writing down. They were angry and disrespectful. When I was finished, I had written three pages, and I felt totally drained.

At the next session I handed him the letter. He gave it right back to me and told me to read it aloud to him. I'm here to tell you that it took me over forty-five minutes to read it. I must have broken down in tears three or four times. When I was finished, he asked me how I signed the letter. "I didn't sign it," I told him.

"Why not?" he wanted to know.

"I'm not sure," I said. He told me to take it home and before our next session add anything I wanted to and sign it.

The night before I was to see him again, I sat down with the letter and added one or two more feelings and signed it. The next day he told me to read it again. This time it only took me a few minutes to do so.

He said, "You didn't read the signature. Do it now." It took me the rest of the session to get the words out of my mouth. The moment I did I saw my life was like an inbox full of neatly stacked papers and someone had just put their hands under it and thrown them into the air. They would never come down in the same neat order. Those sheets of paper were like the events and beliefs about my mother and her death that I'd held for so many years were not what I thought they were. I broke down and sobbed. Coach then told me that everything was okay, and that anger is the first feeling we get when someone close to us passes away. It comes from the fear of the drastic change that is going to take place in our life and the fear of surviving the deep sense of grief and loss. He then told me that next time I would go to my hometown, to go to her grave and read her the letter. He said that the reason I was feeling the way I was, was because when I read my signature, I had given my mother complete forgiveness for what I'd always considered betrayal, in turn I forgave myself for harboring the feeling that she betrayed me. He suggested that I go home and rest as I'd had an emotional morning. The rest of the day I sat in our living room with the television on but paying no attention to it.

Darlene got home from work that evening and asked how it had gone with Coach, and I told her all that happened. When I told her that I was to read it to my mother back at home she simply took my hand and the letter and said let's go. I just followed without asking where we were going. We pulled into a nearby cemetery, and she drove up to a large monument that said MOTHER. I got out, sat at the edge of the large headstone, and read the letter. Surprisingly, it only took a few minutes, and I had no negative emotional/spiritual reaction to the video of her funeral service.

The following morning when I awoke the bright sun was shining through the blinds across the bed and a slight breeze was causing the curtains to open and let the fresh air in. I immediately sat up feeling light as a feather. The first words out of my mouth were, "Oh my God, this is the first day of the rest of my life and no one can take this feeling of peace away from me."

Little did I realize until many years later what I'd experienced was the conversion of a part of my spirit that was permanently negative, controlled by fear to the positive energy of God's spirit of love. I was also to learn that we must work at having peace as the world will continue to attack our positive thoughts and cause our fear to destroy our peace.

Over the years I can't tell you how many letters I've written to give spiritual forgiveness to those I felt did me wrong. Some events will require more than one letter. I've written several letters to my first wife and to my high school bully. The good news though is that not only did I forgive them, Darlene and I became friends with my ex-wife and her new husband. As for the bully, we even got to where we were cordial to each other.

There are a couple of important things to remember. First it is essential that you read the letter aloud either to someone or to yourself. Secondly, reading your signature is critical as it brings closure and releases the negative emotional/spiritual connection to the event or person. Finally, the person you write the letter to must never see the letter. After you read it destroy it.

For me Jesus sent very strong messages as he hung on the cross in total agony. The first was when He called out to His Father to forgive them for, they know not what they do. This message was that no matter how badly we are treated, no matter how egregious the transgression against us we must forgive them.

The second was a message that had two parts, I think most of us missed the second part altogether. At least I know I did until after I stood in the Light. The first part of the message we all know well. Jesus died on the cross to give each of us forgiveness for our sins. The second part is seldom spoken of. The second part is this; when Jesus forgave us that was only half of the equation. The other half was we must forgive ourselves. Honestly, failure to do that, in my opinion, is an insult to His sacrifice. What I've shared in this chapter shows you one way of achieving that self-forgiveness. Always remember that forgiving is more for us than it is to the other person.

Why is forgiveness so very important? Simply this, when we fail to forgive ourselves that negative spirit that we harbor from that transgression will always be hiding in the shadows of our mind and at every opportunity it will show its presence and steal a part of our peace. If you want to experience the maximum level of peace you must learn to forgive.

Chapter 20

Fear

Throughout this book, I've talked a lot about our emotions and how those emotions are, in reality, our spirit which determines who we are as a person, directs our lives, and motivates our decisions. I've talked a lot about God's spirit of love, and its power to make our lives as good as is possible. In fact, the Bible tells us that God does all things for good. I've talked about the right of free choice and the battle of the spirit, which is fought by whether we make our decisions from Satan's fear or God's love. I've touched on the spirit of fear, but I need to share more details.

Just as God's spirit is positive spiritual energy, Satan's fear is our negative spiritual energy, which is Satan's weapon, and is the negative energy of our spirit. It obviously plays a large role in shaping our lives so, it's time to look at fear more closely. The more we understand fear, and how its negative energy affects us, the easier it is to manage it. Don't kid yourself, you can learn to manage fear, but you cannot control fear, and you cannot destroy it. You can only learn how to manage it so that it does not control your spirit and becomes the primary motivator of the decisions that direct your life, which becomes how others see you as a person. We've all heard someone referred to as being mean spirited or the opposite, kindhearted.

There is no such thing as being fearless. Fear is part of your spirit and will always be there. Again, don't fool yourself with contrived bravado. There is a difference between being brave and being courageous.

Acts of bravery are instant reactions to a dangerous situation and are directed by your positive spirit. Acts of courage, on the other hand, are responses, not reactions. Courageous people are very aware of their fear regarding the danger they face but still act, even in the face of that fear. Here are some examples.

We've all heard of the soldier who threw himself on an enemy hand grenade to save his fellow soldiers. This is definitely an act of bravery. The soldier acted without thought for his own life, but out of a deep sense of caring and loyalty to his fellow soldiers. There is no greater love than to lay down one's life for others.

Now, consider those who participated in the Normandy invasion on D-Day. Despite the dangers they faced, and the fear that they felt as their boats approached the shore, they charged out of the boats into the face of massive gunfire to engage the enemy. That, my friends, is a true act of courage. Courage, like bravery, is an act directed by the spirit of love. A love so strong it overcomes fear. In the case of these soldiers, it was their love for their families and their country. You may say, "Well they were in the military and were doing it because of their orders." To a degree that may be true, however, there is a limit to the level of courage one can be forced to exhibit. If you aren't sure of this, look at the number of people that ran to Canada to avoid serving in the Vietnam war. Yes, many conjured up reasons, to justify their decision.

Let's look at the origin of fear. Satan's first appearance was in the Garden of Eden where he appeared as a serpent, but a charming one. Since he lives by no rules, he can appear in any form he chooses. He hides his insidious evil behind charm and appears to be very pleasant and caring, claiming to be the provider of protection from all threats, and the provider of great pleasures. He is very persuasive. Also in the Garden, as the Bible tells us, was the tree of knowledge. God provided Adam and Eve a wonderful life, a life in paradise full of peace, love, and joy and promised to provide for their every need. The only conditions were that they love Him completely, put total trust in Him, and not eat from the fruit of the tree of knowledge. It is also what God has given us. He has promised us that we can live in the spiritual paradise of His Kingdom. But with these conditions we will love Him unconditionally; trust in Him completely; live by His laws, the ten commandments; and not succumb to Satan's deceit, visions of wealth, and false promises.

Satan persuaded Eve that God's rules and restrictions were depriving her and Adam of the wonders of the world. Today, Satan is trying to persuade us that God's laws are depriving us of all the good things life has to offer, and that if we disregard them that he, Satan, will protect you from any consequences. Lucifer was one of God's angels who fell from grace, and it made him very angry. As a result, Satan chose to use his powerful negative spirit to fight God's spirit of love. He constantly plants the seeds of doubt causing us to doubt our trust in God. Life causes threats to our survival and Satan uses these threats to convince us that God is not protecting us, but that Satan is because his fear caused you to react in time to save yourself.

From my personal experience, I can tell you there are consequences. For all my rogue years, I experienced the great pleasure of doing most of the things that are forbidden by God's laws. The point came where fear was controlling nearly eighty-five to ninety percent of my spirit. I learned that Satan was not going to protect me because he only wanted to control me. I promise you; fear is a nasty task master.

Then someone left the door to heaven open, and God put His Angel, Darlene, in my life. For the first time in many years, I was able to see glimpses of life not controlled by fear. As time went on, I discovered glimpses of the peace I'd been so desperately searching for. I also began to realize that the peace I sought was not able to be found in the material world. I realized that kind of peace was only temporary. As I continued to learn from working with the Special Forces counselor, and from my Christian coach, the peace I was looking for could only be found in my own spirit, my own soul. The more I learned to manage Satan's fear, the more peace I felt. Yes, it is true, only fear can destroy peace, and the only true lasting peace resides in our spirit through God's wonderful love. Like all things, God does not just give you peace, it must be earned.

In today's world, Satan has ramped up his efforts to take control. For many years, Satan has disguised himself as a person who was a charming, caring person and in a position of influence. Fortunately, their obsession for power and wealth causes them to come out and show their true intentions. Unfortunately, Satan's lust for wealth and power has become so strong it is now visible to everyone that choose to see it for what it is. As a result, the level of fear being constantly fed to our population has us confused and has rendered us unable to regain our trust in God.

In the Garden, the serpent persuaded Eve that God was depriving her and Adam the knowledge to live the real pleasures of life. Therefore, she should not trust God and should eat from the forbidden apple. She should then persuade Adam to do the same. The moment they had both eaten, they instantly realized they were naked and quickly covered themselves with leaves. Now they were afraid because they knew that God was going to be very mad at them for their betrayal. At that moment, fear was introduced to mankind and marked the beginning of what the bible refers to as the battle of the spirit. Unfortunately, as you have read, I was nearly one of them.

Chapter 21

Managing Fear

So, what causes us to experience fear and how do we fight it to earn God's peace? First, let's talk about what causes us to experience fear, then we will talk about how to manage it, and earn God's peace.

As I said earlier, our basic instinct is the instinct of survival. Not just life or death, but in every area of our lives. Professional, relationships, belongingness, finances, and the list goes on. Any time, when any one of those areas is threatened, whether the threat is real or perceived, fear is the immediate reaction. Now, that's not all bad. When we are threatened by a real and imminent danger, we react, and that reaction can save our lives. It is what happens next that makes fear dangerous. After the immediate crisis has passed, we feel the adrenalin subside, our pulse returns to normal, and our blood pressure lowers to normal. Now it is time to make a very important decision. Remember, decisions are made spiritually, either fear or love. The question we must answer is how are we going to allow this event to affect the rest of our lives? If we listen to our spirit of fear, we decide to never put ourselves in that position again. That fear will control your life until you remove it from your spirit. If we decide from the spirit of God's love, we will hear it tell us that yes, the event was very frightening, but God provided you with a way to handle it. Learn from it and move on with your life. Let me give you another personal example.

In 1962, I was running an insurance debit book for a wonderful company out of Topeka, Kansas. I was working out of Parsons, Kansas but once a month I had to drive to Chanute, Kansas, which is approximately thirty miles, to the regional office to balance my debit book and to get additional training. This was always on a Saturday. In the spring of that year, I was returning from one of those Saturday meetings and was only a short way from my home. As I was coming down the hill leading into town I suddenly couldn't breathe, my heart was pounding, and I had a massive chest pain. I was only 20 years old, so a heart attack was highly unlikely. I was shaking so bad I could hardly keep my foot on the accelerator. I don't know how, but I finally made it home. I ran into the house and only then did I calm down. Yes, that was my first of many panic attacks.

So, when I got home, the crisis was over. I was in my safe space. I was returning to normal, now time for that very important decision on how this event was going to affect the rest of my life. Unfortunately, I made that decision out of my spirit of fear, saying, "I'll never put myself in that position again."

I decided the only way that I could be safe was that anywhere I went, to be in a safe space, was to have someone with me. For many years, thereafter, that decision had a very negative impact on my life and how it affected my decisions. Especially my decisions when it came to being alone when I traveled in my car. In fact, for the next year, I refused to leave my house unless someone went with me because at that time, home was my only safe space.

Of course, this created a problem because our daughter was not yet two years old, so my wife could not ride with me every day. How was I going to do my job and make a living for my family? I called my boss and told him what happened, and he told me he would need to give the debit route to someone else and I would need to leave the company. I then went to work for a company that only sold life insurance. Since I couldn't go out alone, that meant I had to learn to sell over the phone and make enough commissions to provide for my family.

For the next year, that is exactly what I did. I sold over the telephone and the applicant would come by my house and sign the application and give me a check. Yes, it was still a time when people were not as fearful and paranoid as they are today. Honestly, it got to where I was very successful at telephone sales. The truth is, that during that year, I got to where I could determine, by the sound of the prospect's voice, whether they were with me, tolerating me, or getting ready to hang up. I got to where their voice tone let me know when it was time to ask my closing question. Later in life, I learned that I'd developed an ability to read other people's spiritual energy.

I also learned later that in interpersonal communication only seven percent of a message is delivered verbally (words), thirty-eight percent is delivered vocally (voice tone), and fifty-five percent is delivered visually (body language). Words and voice tone were all that I had available. Imagine just how bad communication is now with texts and emails, and where many words are misspelled. There is a real possibility that the meaning of the text or email may be totally misunderstood. Unfortunately, it is that absence of communication, through voice tone and body language, that is absent in texts and emails. This has caused tremendous problems in both personal relationships and business dealings.

This is true because words come strictly from our mind and are mostly void of emotion. Voice tone, on the other hand, is a combination of intellectual thought and emotional/spiritual feeling. I didn't know it then, but now I realize I was successful selling over the phone because I was reading the prospects spiritual energy in their voice tone. Over the years, and still to this today, I am acutely aware of people's spiritual energy.

During that year of physical isolation, something good happened that helped me get past a portion of the extreme fear of going out alone. I was still having difficulty breathing, so my wife took me to the doctor, and he determined that I had some respiratory issues, and he treated me for them. I learned later that I had a mild case of bronchiectasis, a condition where the small air sacks do not empty properly thus restricting your ability to get the volume of air your lungs need to breathe properly. Mine has since been treated properly and no longer affects my life.

As my breathing got better, my extreme fear began to subside to what I accepted as a manageable level. I could go out alone, even though occasionally, I'd get hit with a minor panic attack and needed to rush home.

It's funny now, but it wasn't then. One day I was in the barbershop getting a haircut. The barber had tightened the apron around my neck a little too tight and halfway through the haircut, I panicked. I jumped from the chair and ran out the door and down the street to my car. I'm sure people had a great laugh as they saw a man running with a barber's apron flowing behind him like superman's cape, being chased by an irate barber still holding his clippers.

Unfortunately, it still didn't alleviate my fear of traveling long distances alone, a condition that plagued me until the fall of 1990. After working with my Christian coach for six years, I was able to manage this fear. You may remember, it was January of 1991 that we became engaged in Desert Storm. I had already retired from the Army, but Darlene got activated from her reserve status back to active duty. Thank goodness she wasn't deployed to the sandbox, the middle east, but instead, was assigned to casualty operations in Washington, DC.

At that time, we were living in Powder Springs, Georgia, a suburb of Atlanta, and I'd started my training and consulting company. For months, Coach and I had been working to get me able to take trips alone. At that point my trips were within the state of Georgia. This represented a major expansion of my travel safe space. You may be wondering, with this problem, how was I able to be in the army and do everything else I was doing? That is a valid question. In my opinion, we have many different areas in our life where we can develop a safe space. Usually, the one that caused the first panic attack is the most difficult to deal with. Never, while I was in the army, did I have to travel by car for a long distance.

So, Darlene is off to DC for an unknown length of time; at least three months, maybe more. We were once again separated. Neither of us was happy with that as we'd already lived through that kind of situation while in the army, and we had no desire for a repeat. I solved the problem. We had gotten Darlene a two-bedroom furnished apartment in Old Town Alexandria, Virginia, close to the Metro train station. The Metro, at that time, was the cleanest, safest, and most efficient rail system in the country.

My solution was simple. To run my business all I needed was a small office, a telephone (I was still pretty good at selling on the telephone), and an airport. The apartment had a second bedroom, my office, and it had a telephone. National Airport was only a couple of Metro stops away. We were in business.

I closed the house in Atlanta, packed all we were going to need, loaded the kitties in the car, and backed out of the driveway -- destination, Old Town Alexandria, Virginia, nearly a thousand miles away. As I hit the interstate, I said a little prayer asking God to protect me and guide me. Late that night, I pulled into the parking lot of the apartment building. I'd done it, I'd driven a long distance alone and enjoyed every minute of it.

The point of this story is that once Satan's fear gets his hooks into you, it requires a Herculean effort get loose. But God will give you the strength and guidance to accomplish the mission, just like He did for me, if you will only trust Him. Let me give you another example.

My safe space continued to expand over the years. In fact, in 1996 I had a contract with ATTGIS, a subsidiary of AT&T created by a merger between ATT and National Cash Register. Part of the contract required me to do some work in Bangkok, Thailand. I flew from Atlanta to Tokyo, Japan, changed planes and flew on to Bangkok. I did this by myself and enjoyed every moment of the journey. After three weeks work, I flew home, but by then the airspace over Vietnam had been opened to commercial flights. Our pilot had been a fighter pilot during the Vietnam war, and he flew us the length of the country from north to south at 10,000 feet without getting our feet wet at Da Nang. That was as close to Vietnam as I ever got. It seems God had different plans for me.

Chapter 22

A Usable Definition of Fear

A threat to our survival, very seldom, is an immediate and imminent danger. Unfortunately, we have been programed with a fight or flight response to threats. If it's an imminent danger, this reaction is appropriate. For all other threats, it is not only inappropriate, but it can bring very negative results. So, let's look at how to respond to non-imminent danger threats.

First, we must define fear in a way which we can understand. We've never been taught to understand how to manage emotions and the spirit. So, rather than thinking of it in terms of emotion, we need to think of it in terms of a series of questions. Those questions, of course, are the same every time we are threatened. Am I going to survive; am I going to be okay; how do I handle the situation? You may ask these questions, either consciously or unconsciously, but you will ask them every time you feel threatened.

To earn God's peace, we must learn to reduce the fear side of our spirit and replace it with God's spirit of love. We must learn a new way to handle that important question. Most of us answer the question by saying. "I don't know." That, of course, takes our fear to a higher level because the fear of the unknown is our greatest fear.

We must realize that there are several levels of fear. All will cause us to ask those questions. The first level of fear is concern. It is such a very mild fear that we may not even be consciously aware of it, but we feel unsettled. The next level is worry. We are consciously aware of worry because we start playing unpleasant scenarios about the situation generating the worry. For example, the kids are late getting home from school. We can certainly come up with some very scary thoughts about why they are late. Those negative thoughts elevate the fear level to anxiety. Now we are increasing our negative thinking and trying to decide what to do. There are several options, but we are so confused and uncertain that we are nearly paralyzed and unable to settle on a specific action. If, after a lengthy period, the children are not home, we reach a level of high anxiety, close to panic, and force ourselves to act so we call the police to report them missing. If efforts to find them fail, we reach the level of panic. At that point, we are experiencing actual physical symptoms. The next day they are found safe and sound, and we nearly collapse with extreme relief.

There is one more level of fear above panic, and it has been identified as Post Traumatic Stress

Disorder (PTSD). It was originally applied only to soldiers who had experienced combat. However, it is much more widespread than that. You see, PTSD is initiated by events that cause us to experience a real or perceived loss of control, and feelings of helplessness and hopelessness. Once fear reaches this level, the decisions being made are motivating actions that can be devasting, such as suicide, harming others, and many other very negative actions.

If you've ever experienced an unwanted divorce, forced into bankruptcy, lost a job, or any one of thousands of negative events in your life, you are subject to experience PTSD. As I look back to when I caught my first wife and my friend, I experienced all the symptoms of PTSD. I felt a great loss of control over my life. I felt helpless to change what happened, and any thoughts of returning to what had been a happy life were hopeless. My negative actions were going homeless for months and then deciding to get a one-way ticket to Vietnam.

Unfortunately, in today's world, we are being fed threats to every one of our areas of survival. Basically, we are being fed fear with a fire hose. We only need to look around to see the devastating actions being taken as a result. Here are just a few. The vast increase in school shootings, shootings at parties, drive by shootings, attacks on innocent people, domestic violence, increased use of drugs and alcohol, suicide, and the list goes on and on.

As a faith-based life coach, what gives me the most concern is the number of people who stop me on the street and ask why I appear to be so peaceful when the world is going to hell in a hand basket? They tell me that they have been devout Christians and believers in God, but if there is a God, why hasn't He fixed this mess? I explain to them why I am so peaceful and how to achieve that same peace. I also explain that God gave us the right of free choice when making our decisions. We are where we are today because of a mass of fear-driven decisions, made by people worldwide, and that God cannot counter those decisions. As I stated earlier, the only thing we control is ourselves and the decisions we make. If we want God's peace, we must earn it by maintaining positive thoughts, which keeps God in control of our spirit, thus giving us His peace.

So here is how we manage the fear that tries to control us. Instead of answering the question, 'Am I going to survive?' with a negative thought, replace your answer with a positive thought. Here is what I've learned about managing fear. When the threat presents itself, I now say, "No problem, I will find a way to handle this just like I have my entire life." When I make that statement to myself, fear loses its control over me, and that positive thought opens my eyes to several options without confusing me. I can look at them realistically and make a good decision. Why do I know that this will always work? I know because I've learned that when I quiet the fear, I can be open to God providing me with the actions I need to take to handle the situation. Here is a personal example.

When we were wiped out in the 2010 financial crisis and moved to Arizona, we still had the car, only it was very near to being repossessed. Besides, it had over a hundred thousand miles on it and was no longer road worthy. One evening at dinner, Darlene and I were talking about how we were going to handle the car situation. She told me that earlier that day she had seen an ad by a local Chevrolet dealer talking about a special deal General Motors had on the Chevrolet Cruise. We decided to check it out. When we arrived at the dealership, we met with the finance manager and explained our situation and that our credit score had dropped to below five hundred. He took us to the sales manager and told him to help us pick out the Cruise we would like to have while he was going to see what he could do to get us financed. Shortly thereafter, we found the car we wanted, and went back to the finance manager. He had us confirm the information we'd put on the credit application. By then it was after nine pm, so he sent us home and told us to call the next morning after ten and he'd have an answer.

At ten sharp the next morning I called him. I was nervous but thinking positively. When he answered, he had a smile in his voice. He said for us to get to the dealership so we could pick up our new car. They didn't want the old one, so we just let it go back. Not only did we get a new car, but he was able to get us financed through GM finance at a reasonable rate of interest. The point of this story is this, once you learn to manage fear, it loses its control over you, and lets God's spirit take over.

Remember, God will always make a way where there is no way. Let it go, let God know that you can't fix it, and ask him to show you what you need to do to fix it. Sounds simple, doesn't it? However, life is not simple. What do you do when you can't stop the negative thoughts and just keep getting more frightened?

Here is what I've learned. You can only hold one thought at a time. Thoughts are generated by triggers from our five senses. So, here is how I've learned to change negative thoughts to positive ones. I gave you an example earlier when I was working with my real estate client, and he remembered his trip to France. I'm going to cover it again, because it is so critical to our wellbeing.

Think back to an event in your life that was so wonderful you wished that every minute of your life could be like that event. As I said earlier, mine is seeing my wife walk down the aisle to me on our wedding day. Once you have that event in mind, try to reduce it to one or two words. When you say those words aloud, your sense of hearing will instantly trigger that event in your mind, and you will live it in the present, as the mind does not know the difference between past and present. That trigger will instantly change your thoughts to positive and change the control of your spirit from the negative energy of fear to the positive energy of God's love. Of course, this takes practice and patience.

I pray that what you have read in this book, about how God's spirit of love lives within us, how our spirit directs our decisions, and the serious impact our spirit of fear can have on us, is helpful. I encourage you to seriously consider practicing the techniques I've shared for managing fear. I can guarantee you that once you do, your level of peace and calm will significantly increase. May God bless you with love, peace, and joy.

Epilogue

What I'm about to share with you happened on Saturday, the thirteenth of July 2024 shortly after six PM. I had just finished the last chapters of the book, the chapters on Fear. In it, I explained that our spirit of fear motivates our decisions, and those decisions direct our actions. I also pointed out that, at this point in our country's history, we were being fed fear through a fire hose and it was creating a significant increase in violence at every level in our society.

I had just finished the chapter when my son, Chris called me. He said, "Dad, they just shot President Trump." I was stunned, and the hair stood up on the back of my neck. I'd just written a chapter on fear and violence, and here was a glaring example of what I had written. You may ask, why I was so certain that it was an example of what I'd written? Why was I so sure that this incident was driven by fear? Let me explain.

Since 2015, when Donald Trump came down the escalator at the Trump Tower in New York city to announce his intent to run for President, he had been hounded and besmirched as a human being, claiming him a danger to the country. From that moment on, his opposition tried everything under the sun to paint him as a horrible human being, even accusing him of being an existential threat to democracy. America is not a democracy. We are a republic. Their next attempt was to silence him by trying to send him to prison. The final straw came when a high-ranking member of the administration said that we needed to put a target on his back.

Now, here is a young 20-year-old man, who had been hearing all this vitriol for over nine years of his life. In my opinion, here is what happened. This young man had grown up to believe that this Donald J. Trump was a great threat to his wellbeing, and the freedoms he loved. That fear motivated a decision to protect himself from this threat. This decision became the action of trying to eliminate the perceived threat.

Fortunately, the attempt failed. Whether you are a Trump supporter or not you should be thankful for his life. Although he had a perfect line of sight and was only approximately one hundred and fifty yards away, his shot missed its intended target, President Trumps head. At the instant the shot was fired, the former President turned his head to look at a monitor, and the round pierced his right ear, rather than directly into his head. Only one centimeter separated a wounded ear from certain death.

As he went down, the secret service detail immediately was on him, covering his body. As he stood up to leave the platform, you could see the blood on his face, and behind him was the American Flag blowing in the breeze. He raised his fist in the air and yelled out, "Fight, fight, fight." There is no question in my mind that one of two things had happened in that very short span of time. In my opinion, as President Trump was hit, he either saw, or felt the presence of God. Secondly, that touch with God changed him, and that change would be catalyst for bring God back into our country and back into the hearts and minds of Her people.

Monday of the following week was the Republican National Convention. On the first night of the convention, Trump walked into the building. As he walked down the hallway, to the main arena, cameras were on him. When I first saw his eyes, I knew. I turned to Darlene and said, "He is a changed man, look in his eyes. There is a deep peace, calm and determination. To me, there is no doubt he was in God's presence."

As I watched him that evening, I became more and more convinced that God had given him a mission that fateful Saturday. That mission was to bring God back into our country. During the Republican National Convention, people who you never heard publicly express their faith in God, spoke out about their belief in God, and openly professed their faith. This was especially true in newscasts. Previously, it was like mentioning God and faith by media personalities was strictly taboo. Many of them even referred to the fact he was a changed man, seeming to be more at peace, and calmer. Now it had become common place.

Does this mean our country is healed? Not by a long shot. It only means that the world has now actually witnessed an astounding demonstration of God's power and love. Unfortunately, Satan is going to fight back, and as he always does. He will bring on a campaign of actions and events that disparage God and create seeds of doubt. As he did in the garden of Eden, he will try to convince us that God only wants to deprive us of the greatness the world has to offer and the great pleasures and wonders that he, Satan, can provide.

This dramatic event demonstrated to the world that God has not yet given up on America.

If you look back in history, from King David forward, every great leader has been put in place by God. We must ask ourselves, is this a case of history repeating itself? Only time will tell. However, what is obvious now is that, as the Bible tells us our battle is of the spirit not the flesh. That battle is now clear, out in the open and in our face. In my opinion there is no question, God's spirit of love is much stronger than Satan's spirit of fear. However, we still have the right of free choice. Our personal decision will determine whether we reside in God's kingdom or in the pain and anguish of Satan's fear. That is a place I lived in for many years and believe you do not want to live there. I strongly recommend you choose wisely. "As for me and my house, we will serve the Lord."

May God bless you with the courage, strength, guidance, and love to earn His peace and live in His kingdom.

Testimonials

"Anyone who reads this book will be moved and have a greater understanding of their relationship with God and His working in their life!"
Annette Horner

"Very enlightening. Couldn't put it down."
Larry and Bev Simmons

"Inspirational words of wisdom to refer to often as we navigate life's challenges."
Andrew Robb

Grateful that Nick is faithful to his mission so everyone can come to understand the power of God's love and how to overcome fear and live a fulfilling life.
Jami Tadda

www.ingramcontent.com/pod-product-compliance
Lightning Source LLC
Chambersburg PA
CBHW071017120626
46546CB00003B/1134